Kidnapped

And Other Stories of God's Grace

by

Susie Barnes

KIDNAPPED
Copyright © 2020—by Suzanne Marie Barnes

ISBN 978-1-950398-11-9

Printed on demand in the US, the UK and Australia
For Worldwide Distribution

Dedication

To my Lord and Savior Jesus Christ and to all those who have poured into my life over many decades. I am deeply grateful.

Acknowledgments

I must acknowledge the following:

- Dan and Sherri Colvin, for believing in me and encouraging me to write this book.

- Ruth Mangiacapre, who supported me with her words continually throughout the writing process.

- Pastors Mike and Debbie Sirianni, for always being true pastors in my life.

Contents

*I
know
that
my
Redeemer
lives.*

— Job 19:25

Foreword by
Michael Sirianni

Amazing testimonies come from amazing tests. As you read this almost unbelievable and chilling event of Susie's journey, you'll see how God's faithfulness will turn water into wine.

There is healing and restoration for those who are vulnerable enough to share extremely intimate details of life's most devastating brutalities. There is also hope and deliverance for those who read these details. Susie, a member of New Day Church, is an inspiration to those who have been severely knocked down and feel there is no hope. Her intention is to be completely transparent so you may see that what the enemy means for evil, God can surely turn into good.

I'm always amazed by individuals who have every reason to pull the sheets up over their head and give up, but choose to rise above and refuse to be silenced. Everyone goes through trials, challenges and triumphs in life. Jesus said this:

To him who overcomes I will grant to sit with Me on My throne, as I also overcame and sat down with My Father on His throne.

Revelation 3:21, NKJV

I have gladly written this fore-word, knowing that God will use this little book to set captives free.

Michael Sirianni
Senior Pastor, New Day Church
High Point, NC

Foreword by Ruth Mangiacapre

I have had the privilege of knowing the author, Susie Barnes, for several years now. After watching her life and her faithfulness and steadfastness in serving our Lord, I can say that it truly testifies to the miracle-working power of God. Susie celebrates God's goodness and continued mercy in her daily life and longs for the reader to experience the same.

Having penned such horrific details of her kidnapping, one would only assume she would be left scarred and bruised emotionally for many years. But she wants her story told, for within the pages of this book, you will see a real God who can deliver you from the darkest circumstances. Susie is living a full and abundant life and continues to experience God's favor day by day. It is an honor to know her as a friend and sister in Christ!

Ruth Mangiacapre
Impact Ministries of the Triad
High Point, NC

Chapter 1

Kidnapped: A Miracle of Deliverance

You will not be afraid of the terror by night.
For He will give His angels charge concerning you, to guard you in all your ways.

Psalm 91:5 and 11

He will call upon me and I will answer him. I will be with him in trouble. I will rescue him

13

and honor him with a long life.
I will satisfy him and let him
behold my salvation.
Psalm 91:15-16

Does God have your back? Do angels really look after you? How would you react in a dangerous, life threatening situation? I didn't see this coming ...

"DON'T SCREAM!" the young man commanded as he placed his hands over my mouth from behind. He asked me if I was going to scream, and I shook my head no. Then, as soon as he removed his hands from my mouth, I let out a blood-curdling scream, but at 1:00 a.m., the world was asleep, and no one heard me. And I was right in front of my parents' house.

It was a hot summer night in July of 1974. I had been visiting a friend in a town a short thirty-minute drive from my home. We were watching the impeachment hearings of President Nixon on TV. When it came time to leave, I began the familiar drive home.

Soon I was relieved that I was close to home and could fall

into bed. I was on the last street before reaching home, where I lived with my parents and two brothers. It was a nice neighbor-hood—crime free.

Then, seemingly out of no-where, there appeared a car behind me. One second the car was riding my bumper and the next second it would pull way back. I felt confused as I thought perhaps the driver wanted to pass me on a res-idential street. As I slowed down to let them pass, they attempted to pass me, and it appeared they were going to, but then quickly fell back in behind me, once again following too closely.

As I turned the corner and pulled up in front of my house, so did the car that was following me. The stranger pulled up beside me and began to ask directions to various places, finally requesting that I write them down. As I stepped out of my car, my heart was pounding, as I felt terribly uneasy about this stranger. I quieted my anxiety by rationalizing that I was parked in front of my house and I was overreacting.

The stranger stood behind me as I began to write the directions he asked for. My fears became all too real when he placed his hands over my mouth and told me not to scream. He asked me if I was going to scream, and I shook my head no. He removed his hands from over my mouth, and I let out a blood-curdling scream. But, at 1:00 am, the world was asleep.

He then forced me into his car and kept a death grip on my hand. He began to drive slowly through the neighborhood, stopping once to say that he was looking for a dark street. I was acutely aware of the severity of my situation as every pore of my being was on red alert. My thinking became very clear and methodical. I felt extremely rational in processing my thoughts.

He started the car and continued to cruise the dark, slumbering streets. I knew my best chance for survival was to keep him in the neighborhood. I suggested a few turns (within the neighborhood), and he picked his spot where there were no streetlights and stopped the car.

He was holding tightly to my left hand, so with my right hand I tried to raise the lock on the door to attempt an escape. He quickly slapped the lock back down and gripped my left hand tighter. A short time later, I again attempted to raise the lock, and this time I was successful. In a split second I was able to pull up the lock and kick open the door. He then pushed us both out onto the ground onto someone's front yard, and I immediately began screaming.

He told me to shut up, but I continued to scream. He placed

his hands around my throat and kept telling me to shut up. I fought for breath, but there was none. I was being strangled, and I knew death was soon to follow. My head was turned at a slight angle, and I could see the house across the street. *So this would be the last thing I would see on this earth?*

I was twenty-two and thought about my life and wondered where my body would be found. I felt most concerned for my dad as we were very close, and this would certainly devastate him. *If only I could assure Dad that I would be just fine and for him not to be sad for too long.* I thought about my friends and family, and I hoped they would be okay with my death. I hoped they would take comfort in knowing that I was with God.

Slowly my eyes began to close, as I could no longer fight to keep them open. I said to Jesus, "Okay Lord, here I come." Complete darkness followed.

As I began to regain consciousness , I thought I had been dreaming and had a nightmare and I was really safe at home in my bed. But as I opened my eyes, there was the stranger looming over me ... It was real! I screamed as loud as I could!

Suddenly, a police car appeared, and a policewoman got out. She walked over to where we were in the night's shadows and ordered the stranger to get up. He did not comply, and she repeated her order. On her third command, she drew her gun, and this time he moved off of me.

By then, there were five or six police cars and much commotion in the neighborhood. As soon as I stood up, I was refilled with the Holy Spirit!

The policewoman told me that had I not screamed at that split second she would have kept going because she could not see us in the dark shadows. Imagine what would have happened if I had not regained consciousness at that precise moment!

The officers insisted that I go immediately to the hospital. I couldn't understand why as I felt fine and wanted to see my family. I finally agreed and I would soon find out why they insisted that I go.

Later, I was taken to the police station and my parents were there waiting for me. They seemed very relieved to see me but very serious due to the gravity of the situation. We sat in the detective's office while I calmly gave an account of what had happened.

When Mom and I went to the restroom, I saw myself for the first time in the mirror. ... I said to her: "Is that me?" Unknown to me, my face had been severely beaten. It was black and blue and terribly swollen. I literally did not recognize myself. I later learned from the policewoman that the guy had his fist raised to strike me again when she first ordered him to get up.

Oddly enough, the man was the same age as me. He was married with three children and was AWOL from the U.S. Army.

This whole incident was described by the police as a perfect crime from the standpoint of a conviction, as the guy was caught in the act with many witnesses. After giving my account of what had happened, my parents and I went home to get some sleep.

The next day we were all trying to get back to normal. Little was said about what had happened, but my parents were concerned and seemed to be keeping an eye on me, looking for signs of trauma. My brothers said little, but I sensed their concern. I am so thankful for the family God put me in who gave me unconditional support. That meant everything.

This happened on a Friday night, and by Sunday my face had almost completely healed. On top of that, I was filled with unspeakable joy! I could feel the healing taking place, both physically and emotionally. I didn't do anything to get to that place of joy; it was just there.

Several friends dropped by to see me and one remarked about how happy I was. She had been expecting to find me depressed and, instead, I felt elation. As I began to return to my normal life, I felt a supernatural outpouring of love from my family, my friends and my God. I *knew* that God loved me and was for me. As bad as this experience was, it was worth coming close to death to experience a far greater joy than I otherwise would have known!

There were a few negative repercussions of this event: For weeks I feared that the guy would return to "finish the job." (Even though I knew he was in jail). I was constantly looking over my shoulder to see if I was being followed. I was terrified of strangers. I was afraid of elevators and being trapped. Deserted stretches of road would cause feelings of panic to rise up in me.

The first year after the attack carried the most scars. Over time, the fears began to dissipate. Thanks to the passing of time and God's continual work in my life, I am now free from those terrors of so long ago. The entire incident seems so remote that it is but a distant memory. I have to remind myself that it did happen.

What could have altered my life in a negative way became an

experience that drew me closer to God and carried with it insight and revelation. Part of the revelation was to understand what a privilege and honor it is to know the Lord.

One thing remains: Our life and times are in the hands of God, the One who knows us and calls us by name.

Chapter 2

Saved: The Miracle of My Salvation

You scrutinize my path and my lying down,
And are intimately acquainted with all my ways.
Even before there is a word on my tongue,
Behold, O LORD, You know it all.
Where can I go from Your Spirit?

Kidnapped

Or where can I flee from Your presence?
    Psalm 139:3-4 and 7

All my life I have been plagued with shyness. It is a handicap that I have never overcome. My teachers would remark about it on my report cards. Shyness prevented me from taking part in certain activities, especially if it required being in front of people.

As I entered my teen years in the late 1960s, I began to question everything, such as "Who am I?, "Why am I here?" "What about my future?" etc. At the same time, the hippie movement was gearing up, and one of the main mantras was seeking "truth."

This movement seemed to be just what I was looking for. It wasn't hard to find like-minded people, and I soon became a part of the group. Before long I was exposed to new music, new ways of thinking and the drug culture. This lifestyle was fun for a few years, until it became increasingly apparent that we really weren't looking for "truth" at all, but only for the next high.

Several of my friends died as a result of suicide or overdoses. Others became "burned out" at a young age, and I decided that I wasn't going to let this happen to me. I discontinued all drug use. However, I did keep my old friends. Also during this time, I graduated from high school.

One summer night, in a place where the hippies hung out, we had some unexpected guests. A Baptist preacher and a recently saved musician from a local band came to witness to us about Jesus. They were very brave to approach a group of hippies, not knowing how they would be received. Everyone listened to what they had to say, and no one was rude to them. For the first time in my life, I was told that Jesus knew my name and knew who I was. Even more importantly, that I could personally know Jesus.

Wow! I had never heard this before. Imagine the Creator of the Universe knowing who I was! What a revelation that was! These men accomplished their mission, talking to the hippies that summer evening, and we never saw them again.

Kidnapped

As the summer wore on, I went back to my everyday life and quickly dismissed what these men had said. Soon came the fall and a new school. I began to seek out those who were like myself and soon settled into my group of hippie friends.

There was one unusual thing about *this* group: they had all been saved over the summer and were now walking with the Lord. I began to ask them many questions and I drove them crazy. The seeds the men had planted in me over the summer were now being watered, and I, too, wanted to be saved.

I bombarded my new friends with questions about how to get saved, and I begged them to take me to church with them. It was all I thought about.

Their meetings were held during the week and were in an old building in the downtown area in the next city. They would have to come to pick me up (a thirty-minute drive) and then drive another thirty minutes back to the meeting, then do the reverse when it was over.

It required some planning, and week after week, it didn't work out. I was frustrated because all I cared about was getting saved. I wanted to know Jesus too!

At last the night arrived! I couldn't wait. I was finally going to get saved! I was a happy girl!

When we walked into the meeting that night I saw a large group of people my age standing in a circle, giving prayer requests. The pastor (an older man of about forty) was overseeing the meeting. I don't know what I was expecting, but I was very much aware that I only knew a few of the people in that room. I felt very uneasy in a group of people that I had never seen before. I couldn't believe that they were talking about their feelings in front of each other. One girl was even crying.

People were praying out loud, and I was freaking out as I had never seen this kind of thing before. I was completely out of my comfort zone. Eventually the pastor offered for anyone who had a need to come to the center of the circle. Well, he was certainly talking to me, but to go in front of all those strangers *WAS NOT* going to happen.

Everyone was in the circle holding hands. There was nothing but a brick wall behind me, and there was no way I was going to budge from my safety spot. It just wasn't worth it.

I began to wrestle within myself, asking: "Am I going to leave here tonight without what I came for?" My answer was, Yes. I didn't know that go-

ing in front of people was part
of the deal.

Then a horrible thought hit
me: what would my friends say
who had sacrificed to bring me
to the meeting? They would be
really upset after all the beg-
ging and all the questions I had
thrown at them. Not to mention
all the trouble they had gone to
to get me there that night. I began to feel panic.

Then a wave of peace swept
over me as I had the perfect response: I would tell them, I'm
just not ready. *Whew! The ideal*

response! What could they say to that?

Suddenly, I felt a hand on my back. I was lifted up and gently pushed forward, with the hand escorting me to the center of the circle. I had no choice but to go with the pushing hand on my back.

I was placed down in front of the pastor. To the naked eye it appeared that I had walked to the center of that circle, but I was actually floating and merely moving my legs back and forth in a walking motion. I could swear that I was not touching the floor.

God met me right where I was, in spite of who I was, shyness and all. He already knew every thought in my innermost being. But He loved me enough to help me along and give me the extra push I needed.

The pastor prayed for me, and Jesus came into my heart completely. For the first time in my life, I felt clean and pure on the inside. When I went outside, the stars were brighter, and the colors were more vibrant! I felt as if I were seeing the world in a new light for the first time! Everything changed in a second of time. Little did I know that this would only be the beginning of a life and adventure with God. Things would never be the same again.

There is always more to experience with God, and I have been blessed to experience the "more."

Chapter 3

On Time: The Miracle of Buying a New Home

And my God will supply all your needs according to His riches in glory in Christ Jesus. Philippians 4:19

Some years ago, on the first day of September, my next-door neighbor and friend came over to inform me that she was going to put her home on the market.

We had often discussed the fact that we wanted to move back to the area where we had both grown up on the other side of town. Many of the neighbors in our current neighborhood had moved away, and the neighborhood wasn't the same anymore. If my friend left, I certainly didn't care to stay.

We had always known that the time would come to make the move. This was just the incentive that I needed to place my home on the market as well. After signing with a realtor, I began a new adventure.

The house I wanted to buy had to match both my budget and my desired location. Even though it was a seller's market, for five months there was no interest shown in my house, and it remained on the market. That was just as well, as there was not one single house for sale that fit my criteria to buy.

Every day I would scan the Internet for new listings that perhaps my realtor had missed. Then, after work, I would drive through the neighborhoods in hopes of finding just the right house. Still, there were no homes that would work for me. Those that had potential turned out to be disappointments once we did a walk-through. One house had potential, but it had no closets. In some homes, there were oddly-placed kitchens or bathrooms.

After nearly six months of my house being on the market, there was a sudden surge of interest, and it was being shown more frequently. I was beginning to feel an urgency to find a house to buy.

One house was located in the area in which I desired to live, and from the outside, it appeared to be just right. But it was way over my budget. After my realtor and I did a walk-through, we silently turned around and walked out.

We glanced into the small back-yard, where we saw three sheds and a hot tub. There was not a single blade of grass. The "yard" was completely overgrown and neglected. The decor inside was outdated and in desperate need of a face lift. Another crushing blow to my hopes!

Kidnapped

After six months of being on the market, I accepted an offer that was exactly what I had hoped for. Now real panic began to set in ... where was I going to live? My nightmare was just beginning.

Days and weeks passed without suitable housing available, and I was becoming desperate. The buyers of my house began pressuring me to move. Despair crept in. We had stipulated in the contract that their purchase was conditional on my finding suitable housing, but now the buyers were threatening legal action if

I didn't move in two weeks. I couldn't blame them; I wanted to move too.

My despair and hopelessness peaked on a Monday. Why was this happening to me? Didn't God know about my dire situation? Was I not supposed to move to begin with? Had I made a terrible mistake, one that could not be reversed?

My prayers went unanswered. Darkness engulfed me. Although I was in torment, I continued to go through the motions of packing—as if I had a choice.

Tuesday brought a new day, and with it, new emotions. I felt a joy welling up inside of me that defied logic. I had discussed with my realtor the idea of making a very insulting offer on the outdated house with the ugly backyard. I asked to see it one more time before I made the insulting offer on Wednesday evening.

Tuesday, as I continued to pack, I couldn't squash the illogical joy and excitement that I was experiencing. What was wrong with me? Did my emotions not understand reality?

It was a supernatural joy, and nothing that I could say to myself could stop it.

Then came Wednesday. I felt anxious and full of anticipation concerning the insulting offer I was going to make later. Coming up at 6:00 pm I would have that last walk-through before making the offer.

At 4:00 pm I received a phone call at work from the realtor. She said that the seller was sick of dealing with the house and if I would take it that day at a certain price, I could have it! I couldn't believe my ears! They wanted two thousand dollars LESS than the insulting offer I had been prepared to make! I bought my new home that same day!

What did I learn about my God through this experience?

- God sees the end from the beginning
- God's timing is perfect
- God cares about deadlines
- God is working—even when it appears that nothing is happening

I have been in my house for many years now, and I'm very happy here. There have been many changes made to the interior of the house, and the backyard is my sanctuary. It has only one shed now and rich green grass and window boxes with lots of flowers. God truly gives us beauty for ashes, the oil of joy for our mourning.

Chapter 4

Healing: A Miracle of God's Promise Fulfilled

God is not a man, that He should lie,
Nor a son of man, that He should repent;
Has He said, and will He not do it?
Or has He spoken, and will He not make it good?

Numbers 23:19

Kidnapped

Does God honor His promises to you?

Can His voice be trusted to speak the truth?

What do you do when God has clearly spoken one thing and yet circumstances say the opposite?

To many people, my dad was an ordinary man. He went to war, earned a Purple Heart, came home, married and started a family.

He was of average height, average weight and average occupation. But to me, he was a special person, one I was honored to call Dad.

During one Christmas season when my brother and I were young, Dad declared that on the coming Saturday afternoon we were going to have a Christmas party. He instructed us to go door to door a few days before the party and invite all of our friends up and down the block ... and to tell them to dress up.

Kidnapped

Dad spent the day cooking and baking for our Christmas party. He loved to bake and share his creations with others. All of our friends came that afternoon in party dresses or nice slacks and sweaters. We had a fun day that remains a memory of our childhood, given to us by our dad. I still have the photos to prove it.

As we grew older, Dad always wanted our friends to feel welcome in our home. He set up a pool table and a ping pong table in our basement for us to enjoy with our friends. He loved teenagers, and they loved him too. As the years went on, a few friends even asked Dad for advice concerning their future endeavors. They knew he had wisdom and cared for them.

Soon enough, I was twenty something and not dating anyone. I remained hopeful that I would meet the right man some day.

As time passed, Dad developed some medical issues, and I was concerned for him as I loved him deeply. One night I sought the Lord concerning the future. I asked God if Dad would be alive to give me away at my wedding ... whenever that day came. God said, "Yes." And with peace and contentment in my heart, I went on my merry way, confident of the word the Lord had spoken to me.

Years later, Dad went to see his doctor one day because he wasn't feeling well. The doctor ran several tests but didn't find anything wrong. Just as a precaution, he decided to admit Dad into the hospital for observation. Several hours after being admitted, Dad experienced a

Code Blue massive heart attack. His heart had just stopped. Out of nowhere, nurses and doctors came running in response to the Code Blue. The medical staff was able to shock Dad back to life. For days, he hovered between life and death. Only time would tell the outcome.

Meanwhile, my heart was broken. I was overcome with grief. I kept asking God if He had changed His mind about Dad being there to give me away at my wedding. But Heaven was silent. I KNEW what God had spoken to me years earlier, but now I had to trust the Lord to do what was best for my dad.

I prayed and cried myself to sleep over the next few days. "Why, God?" I asked, "Why did You change Your mind now?" The pain I felt went to the core of my being. The doctors had no answers for the outcome, nor did they offer us any hope.

Several days later the phone rang. Dad had suffered a second Code Blue heart attack. Now I was in complete despair. All my hope of his recovery was completely gone. Once again, Dad was brought back and again only time would decide his fate.

At this point, I told God that I would not be mad at Him if He took my Dad, as I was only concerned with what was best for my Dad. I was prepared for the worst.

Friends and family had gathered to help us through this time. Many days and nights of torment attacked me. I was also confused by the word the Lord had spoken to me. The overwhelming pain in my heart could not be consoled. I had a younger brother who needed his dad too. But through the tears I still had to trust that God would do what was best for Dad.

Then, suddenly, there came a turn in Dad's health. Slowly he began to improve. My hope returned. I couldn't believe what was happening! Dad was actually getting better! God did not change His mind at all! He is faithful to His Word, to perform it.

After a month in the hospital, Dad came home to a "Welcome

Home" banner stretched across the porch by a very happy family. Seven years later, Dad walked me down the aisle.

Only God holds the keys to life and death. It is appointed to man once to die, but only when God says it's time.

Chapter 5

Face to Face with Jesus

Casting all your anxiety on Him; because He cares for you.
1 Peter 5:7

It was while on a band trip that I had an extraordinary experience that I will never forget:

Some of my friends from church started a Christian band after playing with other secular bands for several years. The lead singer had even achieved fame as a singer in a group that had a gold record. As each member was now in a walk with the Lord, they had come together and formed a Christian band. They were invited to minister throughout the South in churches and various other events.

My roommate sang with this Christian band, and I tagged along with her on many trips as the designated photographer.

It was the routine for the group to seclude themselves in prayer before each time of ministry. During this time in my life I was preoccupied with a certain problem I was having that seemed larger than life.

We were at a church near Charlotte, North Carolina, and as usual, the group of us had gathered together for prayer. I wasn't paying any attention to what was going on around me as I was preoccupied with my own concerns. I was consumed with asking God for answers concerning my issue, and I couldn't concentrate on anything else. I was in the midst of passionately seeking the Lord.

Suddenly, out of nowhere, Jesus appeared before me! His face was directly in front of mine, and with loving authority He spoke audibly to me. "Look at Me," He said.

I responded to the Son of God with, "Yeah, okay, but what about this issue?"

Again, with the same loving authority, He repeated His words, " Look at Me!"

Even as Jesus was speaking to me, I was also trying to remember what Jesus looked like so I could tell everyone. Jesus knew what I was thinking and wiped out that memory from me.

As Jesus (in His physical presence) departed from me, He once again filled me with His Holy Spirit. It was in that moment that I saw into the supernatural and saw true reality.

Jesus is more real than this physical world that we can see and touch and feel. Jesus is more real than our own existence, and yet He cared enough about me and my problem to actually show up in person to speak to me audibly!

Obviously, Jesus hears our prayers, and our concerns are His concerns. He really hears and really sees. He knows us intimately and knows our personalities.

Jesus didn't get upset with me that day when I "argued" with Him about not giving me a direct answer to my question. I felt accepted and loved enough to just be myself. After all, Jesus knew me before I was born.

Since that time I've had many occasions to decide what I want to believe ... my circumstances, my own heart, or the Truth, Who is the One Who took the time to come to me and visit me face to face.

*My frame was not hidden
from You,
When I was made in secret,
And skillfully wrought in
the depths of the earth;
Your eyes have seen my un-
formed substance;
And in Your book were all
written
The days that were ordained
for me,
When as yet there was not
one of them.*
Psalm 139:15-16

Author Contact Page

You may contact Susie
Barnes directly at:

barnes.susie@gmail.com

www.ingramcontent.com/pod-product-compliance
Lightning Source LLC
Chambersburg PA
CBHW021213020426
42331CB00003B/344